JULIUS CAESAR

by
William Shakespeare

Teacher Guide

Written by:
Maureen Kirchhoefer, M.A.
Mary Dennis

> **Note**
> Any text of *Julius Caesar* may be used with this guide as references are made by act, scene, and line number.

ISBN 1-56137-303-6

©1999 Novel Units, Inc. All rights reserved. Printed in the United States of America. Limited reproduction permission: The publisher grants permission to individual teachers who have purchased this book, or for whom it has been purchased, to reproduce the blackline masters as needed for use with their own students. Reproduction for an entire school or school district or for commercial use is prohibited.

To order, contact your local school supply store, or—

Novel Units, Inc.
P.O. Box 791610
San Antonio, TX 78279

Table of Contents

Introduction 3

Cooperative Research Activity 7

Reading a Play 8

Synopsis 11

**Discussion Questions, Vocabulary,
Writing Suggestions, and Activities**
    Act I 13
    Act II 18
    Act III 22
    Act IV 27
    Act V 33

Topics for Discussion of *Julius Caesar* 37

Dramatic Plot Map 38

Ideas for Projects 39

Assessment: Essay Topic Suggestions 40

JULIUS CAESAR

Introduction

To the Teacher: The background information on William Shakespeare and on the Globe Theatre are given to use as you choose—either as lecture notes or as supplemental material after students have completed the suggested Cooperative Research project on page 7.

WILLIAM SHAKESPEARE

One of the great mysteries of English drama is that so little is known for sure about one of its most famous playwrights. Fact became mingled with legend in the 100 years after Shakespeare's death, and it was not until then that any biographical information was recorded.

Shakespeare's exact birthdate is unknown, but he was baptized on April 26, 1564, in Stratford-on-Avon, England. His father, John, was a prosperous wool, leather, and grain merchant as well as a town official. His mother, Mary, was the daughter of a gentleman farmer. It is known that young William attended school and studied Latin and literature. In 1582, he married Anne Hathaway, a woman eight years his senior. They had three children: a daughter, Susanna, and twins Hamnet and Judeth.

In 1586, Shakespeare left Stratford to become the stage manager of The Theatre in London, so named because it was the only theatre in town. He soon joined the acting company of The Theatre, and with Richard Burbage and William Kemp he performed at court in many plays.

Shakespeare's earliest works were produced in 1591-92, including several of the histories and *Love's Labour's Lost, Two Gentlemen of Verona,* and *Comedy of Errors.* In 1592, he wrote *Romeo and Juliet.* It was followed in quick succession by *The Merchant of Venice, A Midsummer Night's Dream, All's Well That Ends Well, The Taming of the Shrew,* and *The Merry Wives of Windsor.*

Shakespeare made an important business move in 1599 when he joined Richard Burbage and several other actors and built the Globe Theatre. He was a shareholder in the Globe and a part-owner of a company of actors called Lord Chamberlain's Company, later known as The King's Men.

Many of Shakespeare's plays were produced at the Globe, where he had both financial security and a first-rate acting company to produce his plays. This was his greatest writing period. In 1599-1600 he wrote *Much Ado About Nothing, As You Like It,* and *Twelfth Night.* Between 1600 and 1611, he wrote the tragedies for which he is so well remembered: *Julius Caesar, Hamlet, Othello, Macbeth, King Lear,* and *Antony and Cleopatra,* among others. During this time he also wrote 154 sonnets which were published in 1609. Late in 1608 or 1609, Shakespeare and his partners purchased the Blackfriars Theatre to use as a winter location for play production.

In 1611, at the height of his fame and popularity, Shakespeare moved back to Stratford. His son died at this time. He sold out his interests in London, although he did continue to write and travel to the city until his death in 1616.

The Globe Theatre

Obtain a picture of the Globe Theatre to show your class, or obtain an educational kit and build a small model so students can see the various areas of the theatre as they are discussed in class.

Physical Aspects

The Globe had three levels open to the sky and set on a large platform. The stage jutted out into the audience on three sides. The building itself was octagon-shaped (eight sides). A cross-section of the London population attended. For one cent, a theatre-goer could stand or sit on the ground and would be referred to as a "groundling." Two cents would buy a seat in the galleries and elsewhere. The noblemen paid nothing, and were seated in the lord's rooms near the stage. Plays were always performed during the day, as there were no lights. A flag was flown on top of the theatre on days when a play would be given.

Setting/Staging

The plays performed at the Globe Theatre had little or no interruption. There were no curtains to signal the end of an act, although there was a tiring house, a room where actors could change costumes or stay out of view when they were not on stage. The settings were given through action and dialogue. The actors' soliloquies made the audience feel particularly involved, as the actors seemed to be talking directly to the audience. Actors' entrances and exits were seen openly by the audience through two doors on either side of the stage.

The Actors

Senior actors got the major parts in plays. They were experienced and often held shares in the theatre company. Hired men, who were paid weekly and held no shares, held backstage jobs and played minor parts in the plays. Boy actors played the roles of women and children.

Using Predictions in the Novel Unit Approach

We all make predictions as we read—little guesses about what will happen next, how the conflict will be resolved, which details given by the author will be important to the plot, which details will help to fill in our sense of a character. Students should be encouraged to predict, to make sensible guesses. As students work on predictions, these discussion questions can be used to guide them: What are some of the ways to predict? What is the process of a sophisticated reader's thinking and predicting? What clues does an author give us to help us in making our predictions? Why are some predictions more likely than others?

A predicting chart is for students to record their predictions. As each subsequent scene or act is discussed, you can review and correct previous predictions. This procedure serves to focus on predictions and to review the stories.

Use the facts and ideas the author gives.

Use your own knowledge.

Use new information that may cause you to change your mind.

Predictions:
_____
_____
_____
_____

Prediction Chart

What characters have we met so far?	What is the conflict in the story	What are your predictions?	Why did you make those predictions?

Cooperative Research Activity

Shakespeare's Background and the Globe Theatre

Welcome to the world of Elizabethan Drama! For the next week, you will work in groups to learn the material necessary for a complete understanding of William Shakespeare's background and the environment in which his plays were produced.

Write the names of your group's members below:

_____

_____

_____

_____

Each group is responsible for learning about Shakespeare's life, his writings, and the Globe Theatre. Each member of the group is responsible for creating a visual aid and a handout (outline, notes, etc.) with a bibliography of materials that you used to obtain your facts and that others may consult for more information. Make five copies of your handout.

Now, next to each group member's name, write the topic for which he or she will be responsible

    1. Shakespeare's Life   **2. Shakespeare's comedies and histories**
    3. The Globe Theatre   **4. Shakespeare's tragedies and poetry**

<u>Schedule:</u>

<u>Days 1 and 2:</u> Spend both days in the library researching your topics. Stay in your group on Day 1. On Day 2, work with someone from another group who has the same topic as you do.

<u>Day 3:</u> Spend in class with a member from another group with the same topic. Work together to revise your handouts and visual aids and to practice your presentation.

<u>Day 4:</u> Spend in your group sharing information. Provide handouts and display your visual aid(s).

<u>Day 5:</u> With members of other groups who have your topic, share with the class as a whole the information you gathered.

Reading A Play

Tell the students that when they read a play they must use their imaginations to fill in certain elements that would be included in a novel. Descriptions of the characters and settings must be provided by the reader's imagination and prior experience. The reader must also "play the part" of all the characters, thinking their thoughts and experiencing their emotions. Students should be encouraged to picture "in the mind's eye" what the characters do and how they react to people and events. In short, readers must produce the play "in their heads," relying on the playwright's words, imagination, and past experience.

A play is much like other forms of literature with these exceptions:

(1) The plot is revealed almost entirely through the speech and actions of the characters.
(2) The play is intended to be presented on a stage before an audience, not merely read.

Put the following page, How to Read A Play, on the overhead projector or write the list on the board. If you write the items on the board, you may wish to elicit the students' help and lead them into the responses you seek. Discuss each item. It is suggested that students copy the list and keep it with their other notes for the study of *Julius Caesar.* After reading an act aloud, suggest that students consult this list first and offer their comments before you begin asking questions.

Before proceeding to the play itself, make a chart showing the characters, and keep it displayed in the classroom as you read and study the play. Since many of the names begin with a "C," it's important to preview the names and discuss the relationships between the characters as suggested in the first step of How to Read a Play. A sample character chart is shown on page 10.

When students go to Step 2 of How to Read A Play, "Read the description of the setting," they will begin to understand why imagination is essential. "A street in Rome" has a lot of possible connotations. You can help clarify the setting by asking students to recall what they know about Ancient Rome. Tell them that Caesar ruled Rome from 100 B.C. to 44 B.C. to help them place the play's action in a historical timeline. Have them brainstorm descriptive words for their mental pictures of the "street in Rome" where the first scene will take place.

HOW TO READ A PLAY

1. Look at the cast of characters.

2. Read the description of the setting.

3. Try to get a feeling for the mood of the play.

4. Watch for background information that sets the stage for what is going to happen.

5. Look for the conflict.

6. Discover details and clues that are important.

7. Watch for any evidence that reveals a change in the main character.

8. Try to determine the theme.

Julius Caesar Character Chart

Rome's greatest general, now dictator:	Julius Caesar
Conspirators against Julius Caesar:	Marcus Brutus, Cassius, Casca, Trebonius, Ligarius, Decius Brutus, Metellus Cimber, Cinna
Triumvirate after the death of Caesar:	1. Octavius Caesar *(Caesar's grand-nephew and heir)* 2. (M. Aemilius) Lepidus *(a Roman general)* 3. Marc Antony (Marcus Antonius) *(a young general, Caesar's friend)*
Senators:	Cicero, Publius, Popilius Lena
Tribunes:	Flavius, Marullus
Wives:	Calpurnia *(Caesar's)* Portia *(Brutus')*
Friends to Brutus and Cassius:	Lucilius, Titinius, Messala, Young Cato, Volumnius
Servants to Brutus:	Varro, Clitus, Claudius, Strato, Lucius, Dardanius
Others:	Pindarus *(servant to Cassius)*, soothsayer, Cinna *(a poet)*, Artemidorus *(teacher and friend to Caesar)*, Anstha *(another poet)* citizens, guards, attendants

Synopsis

Act I
Marullus and Flavius scold commoners for taking a holiday in honor of Caesar, and pull wreaths off the statues of Caesar. They have another reason for celebration, however. It is the Feast of Lupercal, consisting of races and games. Caesar, who has fathered no children, tells his wife, Calpurnia, to stand where she can be touched by Antony as he runs in one of the races. Supposedly this will make her fertile. He is superstitious about this, but not about a soothsayer's warning to "Beware the ides of March." Cassius, a conspirator against Caesar, talks to Brutus and tries to find out how he feels about Caesar's growing power and popularity. Brutus is not sure how he feels. Caesar tells Marc Antony that he thinks Cassius is dangerous. Caesar has thrice refused the crown offered by Antony as a ploy to show he is not interested in power. Later that evening, after a terrible storm, Casca tells Cicero of some unnatural happenings he interprets as omens that Caesar will destroy the Roman republic. Cassius, Cinna, and Casca meet to plan Caesar's death, and are joined by Decius Brutus, Trebonius, and Metellus Cimber. The conspirators feel it would be to their benefit to win Brutus over to their cause, and they plan to do so as soon as possible.

Act II
In Brutus' soliloquy, Brutus says he fears what Caesar may become. Brutus is truly concerned for his country and its citizens. The conspirators easily win him over. They discuss the demise of Marc Antony as well, but Brutus is against it on the grounds that they will seem like murderers, not purgers, if they kill Antony. Portia urges Brutus to confide his secret plans to her, but he tells her he will talk to her later. Caius Ligarius joins the conspiracy at the last moment. The next morning, Calpurnia implores Caesar not to go to the Capitol. She has had a dream of Romans bathing themselves in Caesar's blood. Caesar has decided not to go when Decius Brutus arrives. Decius is able to convince Caesar to go to the Capitol by telling him that the dream was actually a good omen. Artemidorus writes a letter of warning to Caesar. Portia, in an agitated state over what she fears may be about to happen, sends Lucius to the Capitol. Her fears are heightened by a soothsayer who tells her he plans to warn Caesar of his own fears for him.

Act III
Artemidorus tries to hand his letter to Caesar as he walks to the Capitol with Antony, Lepidus, and the conspirators, but Caesar refuses to read it. Trebonius lures Antony away from Caesar, and the conspirators put their plan into action. Metellus Cimber pleads for the release of his banished brother, Publius, as a device to get close to Caesar. Brutus and Casca also draw near, and Casca stabs Caesar from behind. The others fall on him, Brutus last, and Caesar utters the now-famous lines, *"Et tu Brute?"* just before he dies. Pandemonium breaks

out. The conspirators plan to explain everything to the satisfaction of the citizens. Meanwhile, Antony's servant appears to bargain for Antony's safety if he comes to talk to the conspirators. When Antony arrives, Brutus and Cassius seem to convince him that Caesar had to die for the good of the country. Antony asks that he be allowed to speak at Caesar's funeral, and Brutus agrees that he may speak after Brutus himself is finished. In his soliloquy over Caesar's body, Antony reveals his true feelings, and he vows to avenge Caesar's death. Brutus speaks to the crowd, easily convincing them of the need to kill Caesar for the general good. Antony then speaks, and convinces them that the conspirators are murderous traitors. Brutus and Cassius, learning that the citizens have been incited to mob violence, quickly leave Rome. Cinna the Poet is killed by the mob simply because he has the same name as one of the conspirators.

ACT IV

The new triumvirate (Octavius Caesar, Antony, and Lepidus) meets to discuss Caesar's will and how they will avenge his death. After Lepidus leaves, Antony tells Octavius that Lepidus is useful only in that he can be easily trained to do their bidding. Relations between Cassius and Brutus are strained as Brutus accuses Cassius of taking bribes. Brutus reveals that Portia has committed suicide, and that perhaps as many as a hundred senators have been put to death by Octavius and Antony. Brutus and Cassius disagree on battle strategies, but Brutus convinces Cassius that they should march to meet the enemy at Philippi rather than waiting to be found. Brutus cannot sleep, and asks Lucius to play music. Caesar's ghost appears to Brutus, tellling him they will meet again at Philippi. Lucius and the others see nothing.

ACT V

The two armies are poised on the battlefield, and the leaders exchange words before the battle begins. The reader learns that Caesar was stabbed 33 times. Octavius challenges Brutus and Cassius to battle. Cassius is already convinced he will die on this day, his birthday. There are more omens of bad luck. Brutus says he won't be a loser dragged through the streets of Rome. Titinius is sent to check on the battle proceedings, and later Pindarus mistakenly reports him captured by the enemy. Cassius, certain of doom, asks Pindarus to kill him. When Titinius comes back and sees Cassius' body, he kills himself. Brutus has been convinced by Caesar's ghost (or his own guilt) that he must die as well. He asks Strato to hold his sword so he can run on it and end his life. In the final scene, Antony delivers a speech over Brutus' body, declaring him to be the only conspirator whose intentions were honorable and unselfish.

Note to the Teacher: *Most students will find Julius Caesar more enjoyable and easier to understand if it is read aloud in class or listened to on a recording. Encourage them to ask questions so that language interpretations can be explained and the action of the play fully comprehended.*

Discussion Questions, Writing Suggestions, and Activities

ACT I

Important Scene: The scene between Brutus and Cassius in the second scene gives important insight into the characters. It shows Cassius' hatred of Caesar and his cleverness as well as Brutus' indecision about Caesar and his vulnerability to flattery.

Vocabulary: Vocabulary words are grouped by scene, with line numbers given after each word.

scene i:	knave 15 plague 55	concave 48
scene ii:	hinder 30 cogitations 50 chafing 101	countenance 38 lamented 55 doublet 261
scene iii:	saucy 12 construe 34	portentous 31

Vocabulary Activity
Before beginning to read each scene, clarify definitions for the vocabulary words by having the students use the words in sentences. Also, discuss which words are used frequently today *(concave, hinder, lamented, construe)* and which ones are used infrequently *(knave, doublet, portentous)*.

Discussion Questions Level I questions require literal comprehension of the play's action. Level II questions require higher-level skills.

<u>Scene i -</u>
Level I

1. Who are Marullus and Flavius? *They are tribunes.*
2. Why were Marullus and Flavius angry with the commoners? *The commoners were cheering Caesar and decorating statues of him, although they recently were cheering the defeated Pompey just as loudly.*

Scene i
Level II

1. What puns or plays on words did Shakespeare make with the cobbler's lines?
   sole - soul, awl - all, re-cover - recover
2. What can you infer about the crowd from the way they are acting in this scene?
   They apparently consider it to their advantage to cheer whoever is in power.
3. Who was Pompey?
   He was one of the original triumvirate members to rule Rome. Jealous of Caesar's success and popularity, he formed an alliance with the Senators against Caesar. When he tried to raise an army against Caesar, he was defeated, and fled.

Scene ii
Level I

1. Who is Calpurnia? (Calphurnia in some texts.)
   Caesar's wife
2. What does the soothsayer say to Caesar?
   "Beware the ides of March."
3. What activity takes place as part of the Lupercal?
   a foot race
4. What does Caesar want Calpurnia to do and why?
   He wants her to make sure she stands where Antony, one of the racers, can touch her as he goes by. This is supposed to make her fertile.
5. Who was Cicero?
   a wise old senator of whom the people have a high opinion
6. How did the crowd react to Caesar refusing the crown?
   They cheered.
7. What did Caesar do after refusing the crown the third time?
   fell down in an epileptic fit
8. What will Cassius do to further convince Brutus to join the conspiracy?
   Cassius will throw several notes through Brutus' window, "as if they came from several citizens," regarding the high opinion the citizens have of Brutus and indirectly alluding to the low opinion they have of Caesar.

Scene ii
Level II

1. What are "ides"?
   In the ancient Roman calendar, "ides" were the 15th of March, May, July and October and the 13th of other months.
2. Caesar is superstitious on one hand, but chooses to ignore the warning of the soothsayer. What do you think this implies about his character?
3. How does Cassius try to turn Brutus against Caesar?
   He sets the wheels in motion for the conspiracy by talking about Caesar's human frailties and Brutus' honorable traits. He talks to Brutus at a time when he is already in conflict over the power Caesar has gained.
4. Why does Caesar want "fat men" around him?
   Fat men are happy and contented in Caesar's view. He feels "lean and hungry" men like Cassius are dangerous.
5. What further information do we learn about Caesar's character from this scene?
   We learn that Caesar has physical weaknesses, that he is concerned about not having a child, and that he has some inclination that there may be a plot against him.

Scene iii
Level I

1. What "portentous things" did Casca report to Cicero and how did Cicero react?
   The omens were a slave's flaming but unharmed hand, a lion at the Capitol, and an owl hooting at noon. Casca saw them as bad omens but Cicero assured him that there is a rational explanation for everything.
2. How did Cassius interpret the unnatural phenomena?
   as signs of the gods' displeasure with the current state of affairs in Rome
3. What characters join the conspiracy in this scene?
   Cinna and Casca
4. How will Cinna help get Brutus to join the conspiracy?
   He will deliver the letters mentioned in the previous scene.

Scene iii
Level II

1. How does the weather in this scene help build dramatic tension?
   The stormy weather lends an ominous quality to the mood of the play. Trouble is brewing just as the storm is brewing.
2. How does Cassius use Casca's superstitious nature to convince him to join the conspiracy?

Casca is concerned about the strange things that have occurred, and Cassius is able to set his mind at rest by explaining that they are directed against Caesar. It is easy to convince Casca that he too should be on the side that is against Caesar.

ACT I Question for Writing: "Caesar" is a word that has become synonymous with strength, tyranny, and absolute power. A person who acts like Caesar is said to have a "Caesar complex." Describe someone you know who you feel may have such a complex. Explain how you and others react to this person.

Activities

• In a small group, brainstorm the word "caesar." Make a list of places and things that include the word "caesar." Decide if the places and things are named appropriately. For instance, if your neighbor has a chihuahua named Caesar, does the dog's personality match?

• To get an idea of how scenes, acts and stage directions work, have the students agree to watch a particular TV program with paper and pencil at hand. Each time the scene changes, they should note the new location and the actors/actresses who are "on stage." They should also include stage directions: movement of the players while on the stage as well as entrances and exits. Commercial messages often herald the end of an "act." Have students take note of this as well.

• *The Roman Record.* Tell the students you will be putting together a newspaper for Julius Caesar's Rome. Each of them is responsible for contributing one of the following to the paper before you are finished with the unit:

- an article summarizing a scene from the play
- an interview with one of the characters or a report of a survey of the citizens
- a captioned cartoon depicting a scene or political idea
- a sports column reporting on the games of the Lupercal
- an obituary for one of the characters who dies
- classified ads, including "Help Wanted" and "Personals"
- display ads for products which would be of use to Romans (for example, an ad for a "toga sale")
- a map of the ancient Roman Empire

Some research will be involved in some of the ideas, so you may want to offer a point range based on the difficulty of the assignment chosen. Collect the students' contributions as you study the unit. Then use a word-processing program to put together your final edition.

• **Lecture/Note-taking Activity.** Put the diagram for PLOT STRUCTURE on the board for students to copy. Explain each step and have the students take notes. Brief explanations for each step follow.

PLOT STRUCTURE OF A DRAMA

4. Climax or Turning Point

3. Rising Action   **5. Falling Action**

2. Exciting (or Inciting) Force   **6. Moment of Final Suspense**

1. Exposition   **7. Catastrophe**

1. **EXPOSITION:** The general atmosphere, time, place, main characters, opening conditions of the play. (Act I, sc. i and ii.)

2. **EXCITING (or INCITING) FORCE:** Something happens that starts the action of the play moving, usually in the first act. (For example, in *Julius Caesar* Cassius convinces Brutus to join the conspiracy.)

3. **RISING ACTION:** This is a series of actions usually covering more than one act. During the rising action, the hero of the play (protagonist) is the active force, making things work out as he or she intended. (In *Julius Caesar*, the conspirators, led by Brutus, make their final plans and Caesar is murdered.)

4. **CLIMAX or TURNING POINT:** The protagonist reaches the peak of his or her power, and a distinct change occurs in him or her as well as in the direction of the action. Things begin to go against the protagonist, who seems to be following a downward path. The climax or turning point usually takes place in Act III or Act V. (In Act III of *Julius Caesar*, Brutus and Antony give their speeches to the crowd. The end result is

that Brutus and Cassius are run out of town and their plans to become the heroes of the empire are destined to fail.)
5. **FALLING ACTION:** This also covers several scenes and shows all the ways the main events are going against the main character. At this time, the antagonist begins to rise in power. The conflict between the protagonist and the antagonist becomes the essence of the play. (In *Julius Caesar*, there is strife between Cassius and Brutus, Portia has committed suicide, and the armies of the two sides are preparing for battle.)
6. **MOMENT OF FINAL SUSPENSE:** Usually found in the fifth act of the play, the moment of final suspense has a particular function in the organization of the plot. Close to the end of the play, it is more significant to the protagonist than it is to the audience. It is the moment when things begin to look as if they will go the way of the protagonist again. He momentarily believes that tragedy will be averted. (In *Julius Caesar*, Lucilius pretends to be Brutus, giving Brutus a chance to escape.)
7. **CATASTROPHE:** This is the complete downfall of the protagonist, either through death or some other devastating circumstance. If the protagonist is a villain, then the catastrophe will be seen by the audience as a good thing. (In *Julius Caesar*, Brutus kills himself.)

Act II

Important Scenes: Brutus' soliloquy in his orchard; the conspirators' argument about whether or not to kill Antony.

Vocabulary

scene i	adder 14	base 26
	redress 57	visage 81
	affability 82	interpose 98
	sufferance 115	lottery 119
	harlot 287	exploit 317
scene ii	valiant 33	augurers 38
	entrails 39	lusty 78
	amiss 83	
scene iv	ere 5	comment 43

Vocabulary Activity

Discuss what the students think the words mean before they look them up. Many of the words will be familiar to them, but they may be used differently in the play. Discuss these differences as you read.

Discussion Questions

<u>Scene i</u>
Level I

1. Who is Lucius?
   a servant boy in Brutus' house
2. What reasons does Brutus have for thinking it might be necessary to get rid of Caesar?
   He fears Caesar will become a tyrant if he is crowned.
3. What was the purpose of planting notes for Brutus to find?
   He would think that many Romans were behind him.
4. Who came to visit Brutus in his orchard?
   the conspirators
5. Name all of the conspirators.
   Brutus, Cassius, Casca, Decius, Trebonius, Metellus Cimber, Cinna, Caius Ligarius
6. Cassius wants the conspirators to swear they will go through with the plan to kill Caesar. What does Brutus say?
   He wants no oaths, only their word.
8. Why do the conspirators fear Caesar may decide not to go to the Capitol?
   They know he is sometimes superstitious and that he was told to beware the ides of March.
9. Explain the discussion about Cicero.
   Cassius feels the inclusion of Cicero in the conspiracy would give them credibility with the citizens, who regard Cicero highly. Brutus does not want to include Cicero because he says Cicero is not a good follower of what others initiate.
10. Who is Portia?
    Brutus' wife
    What does she ask Brutus?
    to tell her what secrets he is keeping
    What does he say?
    He says he'll tell her later.
11. Who is Ligarius?
    He is the last man to join the conspiracy.

Scene i
Level II

1. Give an example from more recent history of a leader popular with the people who later became tyrannical.
   Hitler, Lenin, Castro
2. Why would Brutus be against including someone like Cicero who "will not follow anything that other men begin"?
   He didn't want anyone interfering with his ideas for the conspiracy.
3. Why do you think Brutus did not want the conspirators to swear oaths to kill Caesar?
   He felt no oaths should be necessary among honorable, honest Romans.
4. Which lines tell how Brutus thinks the Roman citizens would regard them if they killed Antony as well as Caesar?
   Lines 162-183, especially "Let's be sacrificers, but not butchers, Caius."
5. Of what proof of her devotion does Portia remind Brutus?
   a self-inflicted wound in her thigh

Scene ii
Level I

1. Why does Calpurnia tell Caesar not to go to the Capitol?
   She has had a dream of Romans bathing in his blood.
2. What did the augurers advise?
   Caesar should not leave his house.
3. Who convinces Caesar to go to the Capitol?
   Decius
   How?
   He explained away Calpurnia's dream as a good omen.

Scene ii
Level II

1. What makes it fairly easy for Decius to convince Brutus to go to the Capitol?
   Caesar has already referred to himself as more dangerous than danger and as terrible as a lion. Such a superman would hardly want to admit to being afraid to leave his own house.

Scene iii
Level I

1. Who is Artemidorus and what has he done?

He is a citizen who is friendly to Caesar and has written him a letter warning him of what will happen.

Scene iii
Level II

1. How does this brief scene create suspense?
   It's possible that the conspiracy's plan is no longer a secret. Caesar may be warned in time and avoid being killed.

Scene iv
Level I

1. Why does Portia send Lucius to the Capitol?
   She is afraid of what may be happening there.

Scene iv
Level II

1. Did Brutus ever have a chance to tell Portia about the assassination plans?
   no
   Do you think Shakespeare wants us to think he did?
2. Why does Portia act like nothing is wrong, and tell Lucius to simply go to the Capitol and come back?
   She doesn't want to show that she thinks something might be wrong.

ACT II Question for Writing: What else is going on or may be going on while Portia is talking to Lucius? What might happen that would change the course of the play?

Activities

- Discuss the following terms with your students. They should be able to define the terms and give examples of each from the first two acts of *Julius Caesar*.

| opening situation | inciting incident | foreshadowing |
| protagonist | antagonist | quotation |

In your discussion of *quotation,* point out that there are many famous lines from Shakespeare which are often quoted. Have them think of lines from other Shakespeare plays they may have studied. Some examples are "To be or not to be..." (Hamlet), "Out, out damn spot!" (Macbeth), and "Romeo, Romeo, wherefore art thou, Romeo?" (Romeo and Juliet)

- Soothsayers, omens, augurers, supernatural events—these are all important in *Julius Caesar.* Have the students give examples of tellers of the future who still abound in our modern world (astrologers, psychics, fortune-tellers) and of supernatural events which have been reported (UFO sightings, ESP experiences). You might ask for students' experiences, opinions, etc. regarding these things. You can also use this activity as a writing assignment, and read students' papers anonymously to get a discussion started. It's important to relate your discussion to the play. Since the class will probably divide into "believers" and "non-believers," you can point out that the same was true in Rome. Caesar himself believed in omens, but felt it wasn't really "manly" to do so. The well-respected senator, Cicero, was a rational thinker.

- Discuss the meaning of this famous quote: "Cowards die many times before their deaths;/ The valiant never taste of death but once."

ACT III

Important Scenes: the stabbing of Caesar; Antony's soliloquy over Caesar's body; funeral orations to Caesar by Brutus and Antony

Vocabulary

scene i	puissant 33	couchings 36
	repealing 51	enfranchisement 57
	Olympus 74	credit 191
	corse 199	Havoc 273
scene ii	lovers 13	extenuated 40
	coffers 91	meet 151
	vesture 198	

Vocabulary Activity

Provide graph paper for students to make crossword puzzles using the vocabulary words. They should write a question or clue for each word, and make a separate copy of the puzzle with the answers. Collect and check the puzzles, keeping the answer keys, and then distribute them to other students to work out.

Discussion Questions

<u>Scene i</u>
Level I

1. What does Metellus Cimber ask Caesar?
   For the release of his banished brother, Publius.
2. Who stabs Caesar first? *Casca*
3. Who stabs Caesar last? *Brutus*
4. Why do Cassius and Brutus say they did Caesar a favor by killing him?
   They say he had less time to fear death.
5. After the assassination, Mark Antony sends his servant to talk to Brutus. Why?
   Antony wanted to be sure it was safe for him to come and talk to the conspirators.
6. What does Mark Antony ask of the conspirators?
   to be allowed to deliver a funeral oration for Caesar
   Who agrees? *Brutus*
   Who disagrees but goes along? *Cassius*
7. What does Mark Antony predict will happen because of Caesar's death?
   "Domestic fury and fierce civil strife/Shall cumber all the parts of Italy."
8. Who is Octavius Caesar?
   Julius Caesar's grand-nephew and heir
9. What does Antony tell Octavius' servant?
   He tells him to relate what has happened and to have Octavius stay away until it is safe to come to Rome.

<u>Scene i</u>
Level II

1. From his dying statement, what can you infer about Caesar's reaction to his assassination?
   He was not surprised that the others were involved, but he was astonished that his friend Brutus had also betrayed him.

© Novel Units, Inc   All rights reserved

2. What is your reaction to Cassius' and Brutus' statement that they saved Caesar twenty years' fear of death?
3. Find lines that indicate Antony agrees with the conspirators. (183-190, 218-220)
4. When do we find out how Antony really feels? (lines 224-275)

Scene ii
Level I

1. In Brutus' funeral speech, what reason does he give for the death of Caesar?
   He tells the citizens Caesar was killed because he was too ambitious.
2. What does Brutus say would have happened to the people if Caesar had remained alive and in power?
   They would all have become slaves.
3. Who does Brutus say are the only ones the conspirators offended by killing Caesar?
   anyone who does not love Rome
4. How do the people react to Brutus' speech?
   They want to crown him as their leader. They believe everything he says and accept his explanation.
5. What does Brutus volunteer to do if the people desire it?
   kill himself
6. Brutus asks a favor of the people. What is it?
   to stay and listen to what Antony has to say
7. How do the people react to Antony's speech?
   By the time he is finished, they want revenge for Caesar's death.

Scene ii
Level II

1. What does Antony say happens to the good that men do after they die? What happens to the evil? Do you agree?
   Antony says: "The evil that men do lives after them,/ The good is oft interred with their bones." Students should think of examples of ways this is or is not true.
2. What things does Antony point out that show Caesar was <u>not</u> ambitious?
   He replenished the public treasury with ransoms and refused the crown.
   Does he actually come out and *say* that Caesar was not ambitious? *no*
   How does he get the crowd to see things his way?
   By letting them draw their own conclusions from the information he gives them.

3. How does Antony appeal to the people's greed?
   He refers to Caesar's will several times to whet their curiosity, then finally tells them what is in the will as the "clincher."
4. How do lines 171-199 affect the crowd?
   (Analyze this section line by line.)
5. What does Antony keep saying about the conspirators?
   that they are honorable
6. Who arrives in Rome at the end of this scene, after Antony's speech?
   Octavius Caesar
7. What did Brutus and Cassius do while Antony was speaking?
   They rode "like madmen" out of Rome.
   What do you think they said to one another as they left town?

Scene iii
Level I

1. Who is the Cinna in this scene?
   a poet

2. What happens to him?
   The crowd kills him because he has the same name as one of the conspirators.

Scene iii
Level II

1. Why do you think Shakespeare included this scene in the play?
   to show the degree to which Antony had incited the crowd—they are now operating under mob rule
2. Give an example of "mob rule" from modern life.

Act III Question for Writing: Antony said, "I am no orator, as Brutus is." Do you agree? Explain your answer by comparing the techniques used by the two speakers to try to win the crowd to their way of thinking.

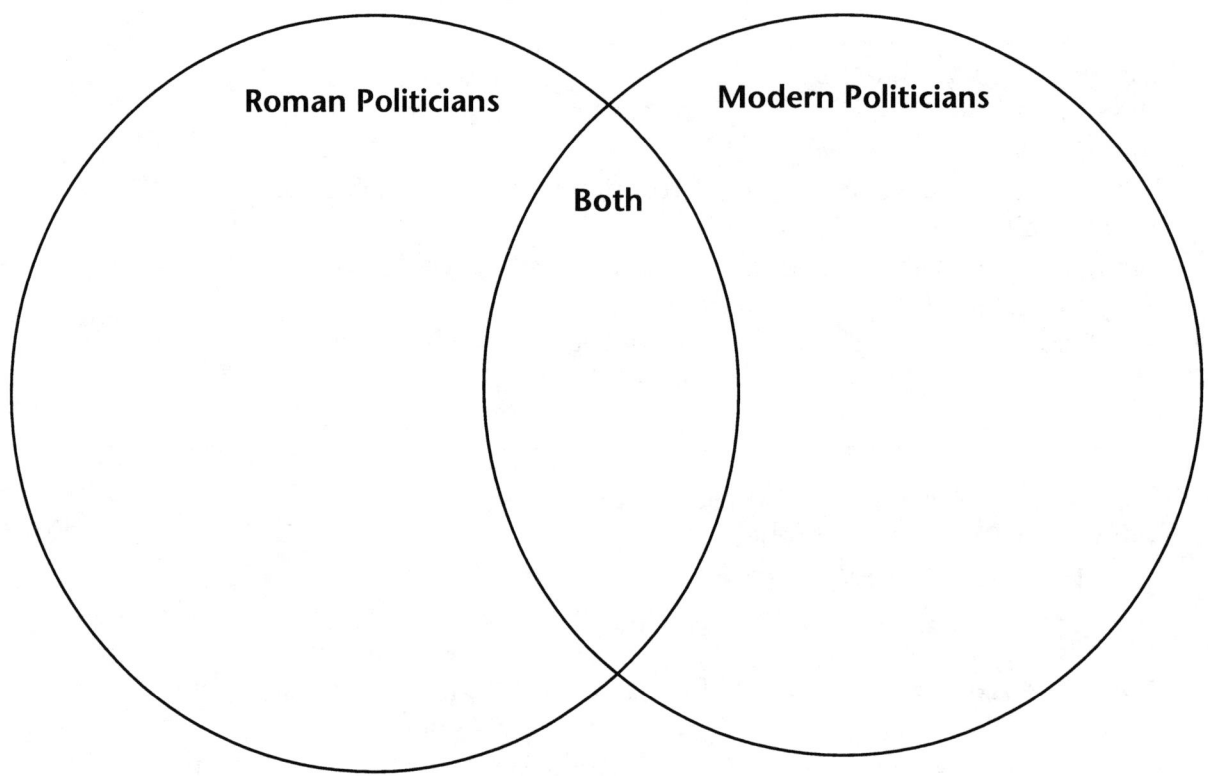

Have the students consider the following when completing the diagram:

1. What motivated Roman politicians? What motivates modern politicians?
2. Discuss and list methods used to obtain goals.
3. List items unique to Romans or modern politicians in their circles.
4. List items both groups have in common in the overlapping area.

Activities

- "Friends, Romans, countrymen, lend me your ears;" is a famous line from this play. Antony used it to get the attention of the crowd while giving them a feeling of kinship with him. Have the students write sample lead-ins for speeches that would address various groups:
    - a nursery school class
    - the student body
    - a panel of teachers
    - a civic group
    - a church congregation

- Both Brutus and Antony tried to "sell" the crowd their image of Caesar. In recent years, modern politicians have engaged in advertising campaigns that can only be called "muck-raking" in order to secure the votes of the American people. Make a Venn diagram on the board (see page 24) and compare modern politicians with Brutus and Antony. Consider motives, goals, and methods. You can also use a Venn diagram to compare the speeches of Antony and Brutus.

ACT IV

Important Scenes: the argument between Brutus and Cassius in scene three; Cassius' death speech

Vocabulary

scene i	provender 30	corporal 33
	covert 46	
scene ii	mettle 24	jades 26
scene iii	vaunting 52	rived 83
	insupportable 150	taper 163

Vocabulary Activity

For each vocabulary word, have the students do the following: find a synonym and an antonym, use the word in a sentence, and find examples from life to show they have a working knowledge of the word's meaning.

Discussion Questions

<u>Scene i</u>
Level I

1. A second triumvirate has been formed. Of whom does it consist?
   Mark Antony, Octavius, and Lepidus
2. What are the three new rulers planning to do?
   kill anyone who was involved in the plot to kill Caesar
3. What does Antony say about Lepidus after he leaves?
   that he is only fit to be an errand boy, not a member of the triumvirate

<u>Scene i</u>
Level II

1. In this scene, we see a different side of Antony. What does he say that seems out of character with the simple and honest man he seemed to be in the previous act?
   He has no problem agreeing that his nephew should die. He is trying to figure out a way to reduce the amount of money in Caesar's bequest to the citizens; he talks about Lepidus behind his back in a superior way.

<u>Scene ii</u>
Level I

1. Who is Lucilius?
   This is another name for Lucius, Brutus' servant.
2. Who is Pindarus?
   Cassius' servant.
3. What does Lucilius say about the way Cassius treated him?
   He was courteous but not very friendly.

<u>Scene ii</u>
Level II

1. What does Brutus mean by a friend who is cooling using an "enforced ceremony"? Give an example from your life.
2. When Brutus realized Cassius was angry, what did he urge him not to do?
   fight in front of the soldiers

Scene iii
Level I

1. Why is Cassius angry?
   Brutus refused to drop bribery charges against Lucius Pella even though Cassius wrote letters on Lucius' behalf.
2. Of what does Brutus accuse Cassius?
   of taking bribes himself
3. What did Brutus ask Cassius for that he has not received?
   gold to pay the soldiers
4. What does Cassius offer to let Brutus do? Why?
   Cassius offers to let Brutus kill him, saying that his life is more precious than the gold Brutus accuses him of taking.
5. What is really bothering Brutus?
   Portia has committed suicide.
6. The night before Cassius and Brutus plan to fight the forces of Octavius and Antony, what disturbs the sleep of Brutus?
   Caesar's ghost
7. What warning is given to Brutus?
   Caesar will see him at Philippi

Scene iii
Level II

1. What reasons does Cassius give for the army not marching to Philippi?
   If they wait until the enemy comes to them, the enemy soldiers will be tired.
2. Why do you think Cassius goes along with Brutus' plan to march?
3. Explain why you think Portia killed herself.
4. Why do you think Shakespeare included this scene in the play?

Act IV Question for Writing: Brutus describes the signs of a "hot friend cooling" to Lucilius when they speak of Cassius. Write your own list of signs of a friendship or other relationship "cooling off." Then write the list in blank verse.

Activities

- **Character Webs:** By now, your students are well-acquainted with the major characters in *Julius Caesar*. Character webs are a good alternative to descriptive paragraphs about characters, or can be used to organize students' ideas before writing a character sketch. Before your class reads the last act of the play, have the students complete character webs for Brutus, Cassius, and Antony and any other characters you feel are important enough to be included. Two outlines for the webs are on pages 29 and 30. You can also use this as a whole-class chalkboard activity.

- **Predictions.** If the students have been using the prediction charts suggested at the beginning of the guide, now is a good time to review them in class. If the charts have not been used, elicit predictions from the students of what could happen in Act V. List them on the board. Then discuss each prediction in terms of how it would affect the main characters if it happened. While you're discussing outcomes of what *may* happen, you might also review the cause-and-effect structure of the play up to this point:

    What caused Cassius to hate Caesar? What effect did this have?

    What caused Brutus to join the conspiracy? What effect did this have?

    What caused Caesar to go to the Capitol on the day he was killed?
    What effect did this have?
    What might have happened if he hadn't gone?
    What might have happened if he had read Artemidorus' letter?

    What caused to crowd to turn against Brutus and Cassius?
    How might the outcome have been different?

- **Speaker/Translator.** Have the students work in pairs for the speaker/translator activity. Most of them will have seen leaders of foreign countries speak on television, with a translator giving an interpretation after every few sentences. Have each student pair choose a speech of at least ten lines from any of the first four acts. Allow them ten to fifteen minutes to compose a very modern version of the speech. Then the pairs can present their speech to the class, with one student reading the Shakespearean lines and the other giving the "translation" into modern language. Encourage the students to have fun with this activity. The modern speech could be a rap song, a valley-girl version, or anything else that is in vogue.

Attribute Web

The attribute web below is designed to help you gather clues the author provides about what a character is like. Fill in the blanks with words and phrases which tell how the character acts and looks, as well as what the character says and what others say about him or her.

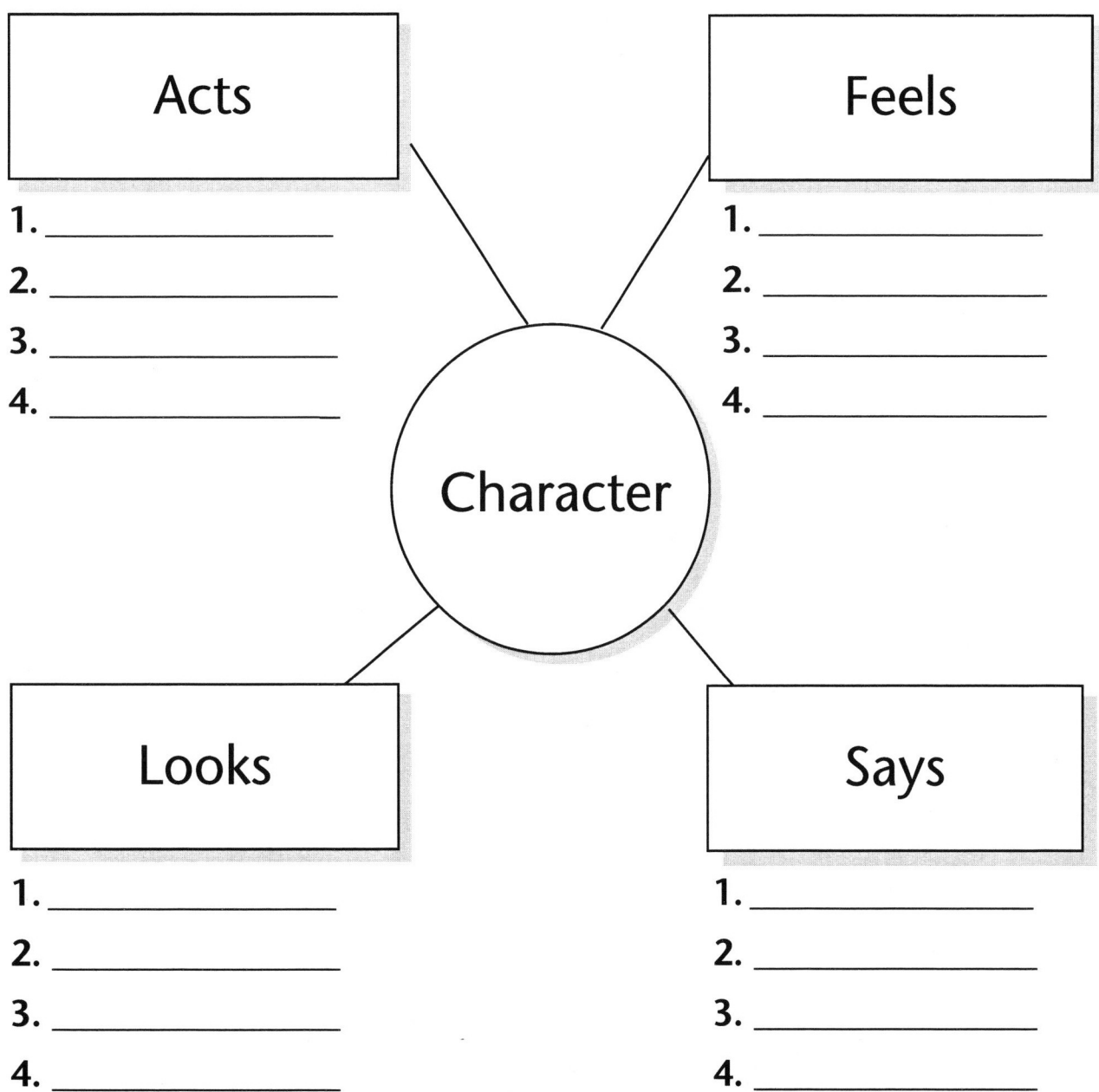

Attribute Web

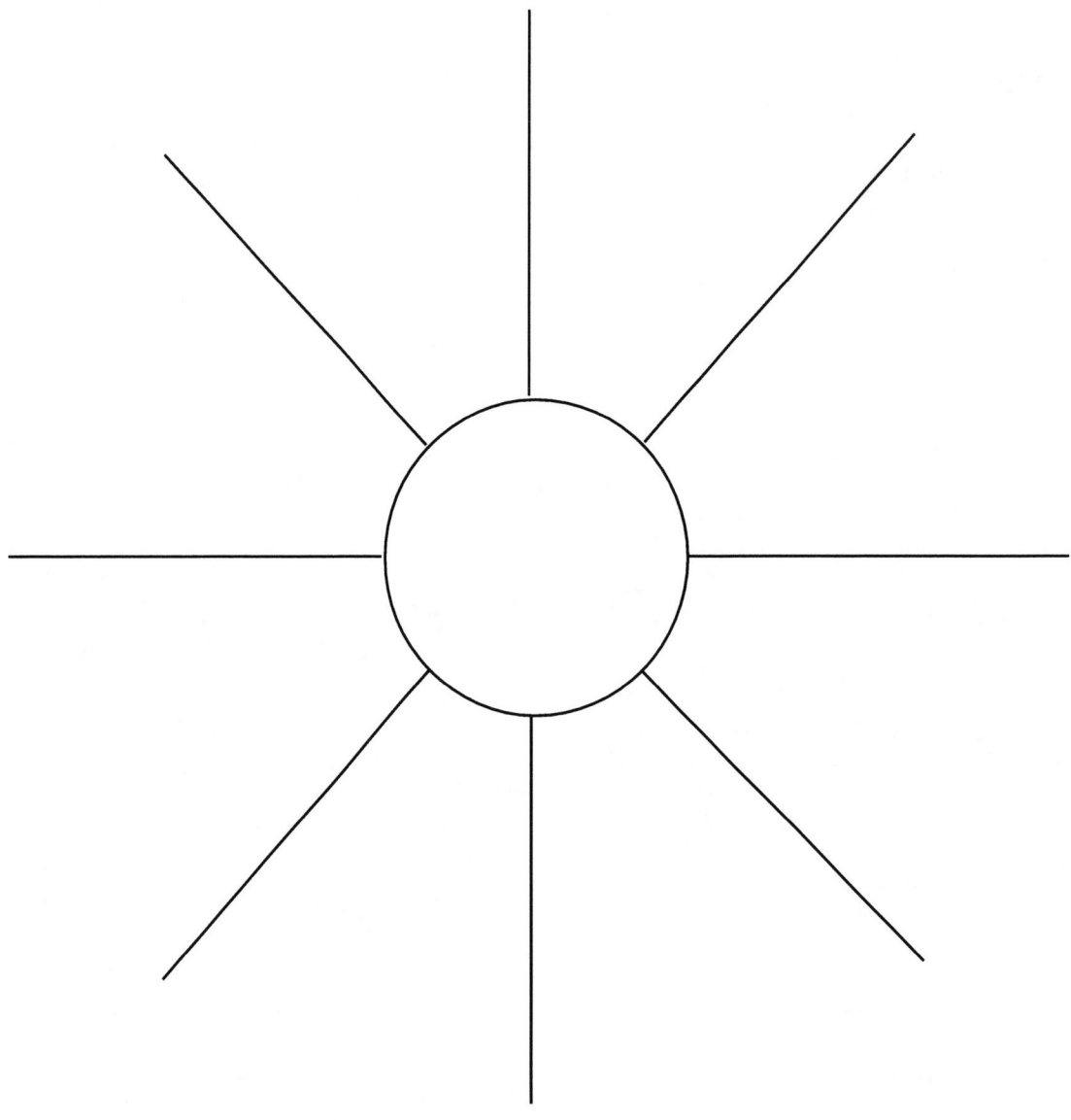

ACT V

Important Scenes: Brutus' death; Antony's speech over Brutus' body.

Vocabulary

      scene iii   disconsolate 55   misconstrue 84

Discussion Questions

<u>Scene i</u>
Level I

1. How many times was Caesar stabbed?
   33
2. Why does Brutus tell Octavius, "Young man, thou coulds't not die more honorable"?
   Brutus still maintains that killing Caesar was an honorable thing to do.
3. What new omens does Cassius report to Messala?
   Scavenging birds are accompanying their armies, waiting to eat the dead bodies.

<u>Scene i</u>
Level II

1. Why do you think Shakespeare included this scene?
   It allows the reader to see what motivates the characters and how they feel about the coming battle.
2. What is Cassius' prediction of the outcome of the battle?
   He is not totally confident of victory for the troops. Although he is a rational thinker, the omens bother him.
3. How does Brutus feel about suicide in general?
   He is a Stoic, and finds sucide a cowardly way out.
4. What does Brutus pledge he will never do?
   Be led through the streets of Rome by a triumphant Antony and Octavius.

Scene ii
Level II

1. What effect does this brief scene have?
   It lets us know there is a possibility that Brutus' army will defeat Octavius'. Also, it shows that Brutus is acting hastily and has not discussed with Cassius this decision to move in his army.

Scene iii
Level I

1. What does Cassius tell Titinius to do?
   Ride down to see if the troops nearby are friends or enemies.
2. What is Pindarus supposed to do?
   He is to ascend the nearest hill and report the action to Cassius.
3. How does Pindarus misinterpret what he sees?
   He thinks Titinius has been taken by the enemy when it is really friendly troops that encircle him.
4. What does Cassius then have Pindarus do?
   kill him with the same sword that stabbed Caesar
5. What does Titinius do when he finds Cassius' body?
   He crowns him with a victory wreath and then kills himself.

Scene iii
Level II

1. How is the action in this scene an excellent example of dramatic irony?
   Because of Brutus' snap decision to send his troops out and try to win, both Cassius and Titinius are dead. It is also ironic that Brutus and other admirers of Cassius profess this admiration only after he is dead.
2. How does Caesar's ghost enter into the action in this scene?
   Caesar is still in the minds and consciences of Brutus and Cassius, and they both refer to him. Cassius says, "Caesar, thou art revenged." Brutus says, "Oh Julius Caesar, thou art mighty yet."

Scene iv
Level I

1. How does Lucilius keep from being killed?
   He says he is Brutus, and the soldiers would not kill such a "noble prisoner."

Scene iv
Level II

1. Why does Antony instruct the soldiers to treat Lucilius well?
   He admires him for his bravery and his loyalty to Brutus.

Scene v
Level I

1. What does Strato do for Brutus?
   Holds a sword so Brutus may run on it and kill himself.

Scene v
Level II

1. Why does Brutus say, "Caesar, now be still; I killed not thee with half so good a will."
   He is more willing to die himself than he was to kill Caesar.
2. What does Antony say about Brutus when he finds him dead? Why?
   Antony calls Brutus "the noblest Roman of them all. He praises Brutus for his honorable motives, and says he was the only one of the conspirators who truly thought he was acting for the common good.

Act V Question for Writing: Explain the major conflicts of the play and how they were resolved.

Activities

- In a novel, there are often titles for the chapters. Reading them before you read the novel gives you an idea of what the book is about, and rereading them later reminds you of the important events of the story. Have the students write titles for the five acts of *Julius Caesar*, and a brief note about the action occuring in each scene.

• Have the students complete the Plot Map on page 36. Discuss the maps after completion.

Activities for Review

• **Final Exam Review:** Divide the students into five groups. Each group will be responsible for formulating questions about one of the play's acts. After the groups have met and written out their questions and a separate answer sheet, have them trade questions with another group. Group members then work together to answer the questions, checking the answer sheet when they have finished.

• **Vocabulary Review:** Divide the class into two baseball teams. Have one student from each team come up to the board to be the opposite team's scorekeeper. Each scorekeeper should draw a baseball diamond on the board with squares for the bases. The teacher asks a student on Team A to define a vocabulary word. If the student answers correctly, the scorekeeper darkens in first base. If the student answers incorrectly, the scorekeeper records an "OUT" on the board. Team A continues to answer questions until there are three outs, and as the "runners" advance bases, the scorekeeper also keeps track of the team's runs. The team with the most runs at the end of class is the winner, provided both teams have had the same number of "ups."

• *The Roman Record:* If you chose to complete the newspaper activity suggested after Act I, it is a good review tool and a way to get parents involved if students take the paper home. Parents who see the newspaper will most likely ask for a synopsis of the play. Students from other classes may also be interested in the newspaper.

Topics for Discussion of *Julius Caesar*

(1) What is the theme? (Ask students to prove or refute the following possible themes.)

- power/disorder corrupt
- evil action, though motivated by honesty, leads to disaster
- bloodshed brings about more bloodshed
- an idealist in a realistic world will fail

(2) Who is the tragic hero?

- Definition: an essentially good person who, through some weakness of character or error in judgement brings doom upon himself.
- must discover the truth of his wrong choice and accept responsibility for his actions
- choice that brought about failure must have been made to bring about results opposite to what really happens
- must be a more admirable man in defeat than he was before; must gain stature through the way he meets catastrophe
- moves the audience to pity
- tragic events happen to a person of great magnitude

(3) Shakespeare's universality— Why is the story of Brutus still intriguing readers today?

- Discuss power and ambition. (politics, power plays, propaganda)
- If your students are familiar with George Orwell's *Animal Farm*, discuss the concept, "Power corrupts, and absolute power corrupts absolutely."

(4) Symbolism/Chief Images

- Discuss the main elements of symbolism in the play: omens, storms, blood, fire

(5) Drama Form: comedy, farce, tragedy, melodrama

Students will readily recognize that *Julius Caesar* is not a comedy or a farce. Read them the following definitions of **tragedy** and **melodrama**, and let them decide into which category the play falls.

Dramatic Plot Map (Melodrama or Tragedy)

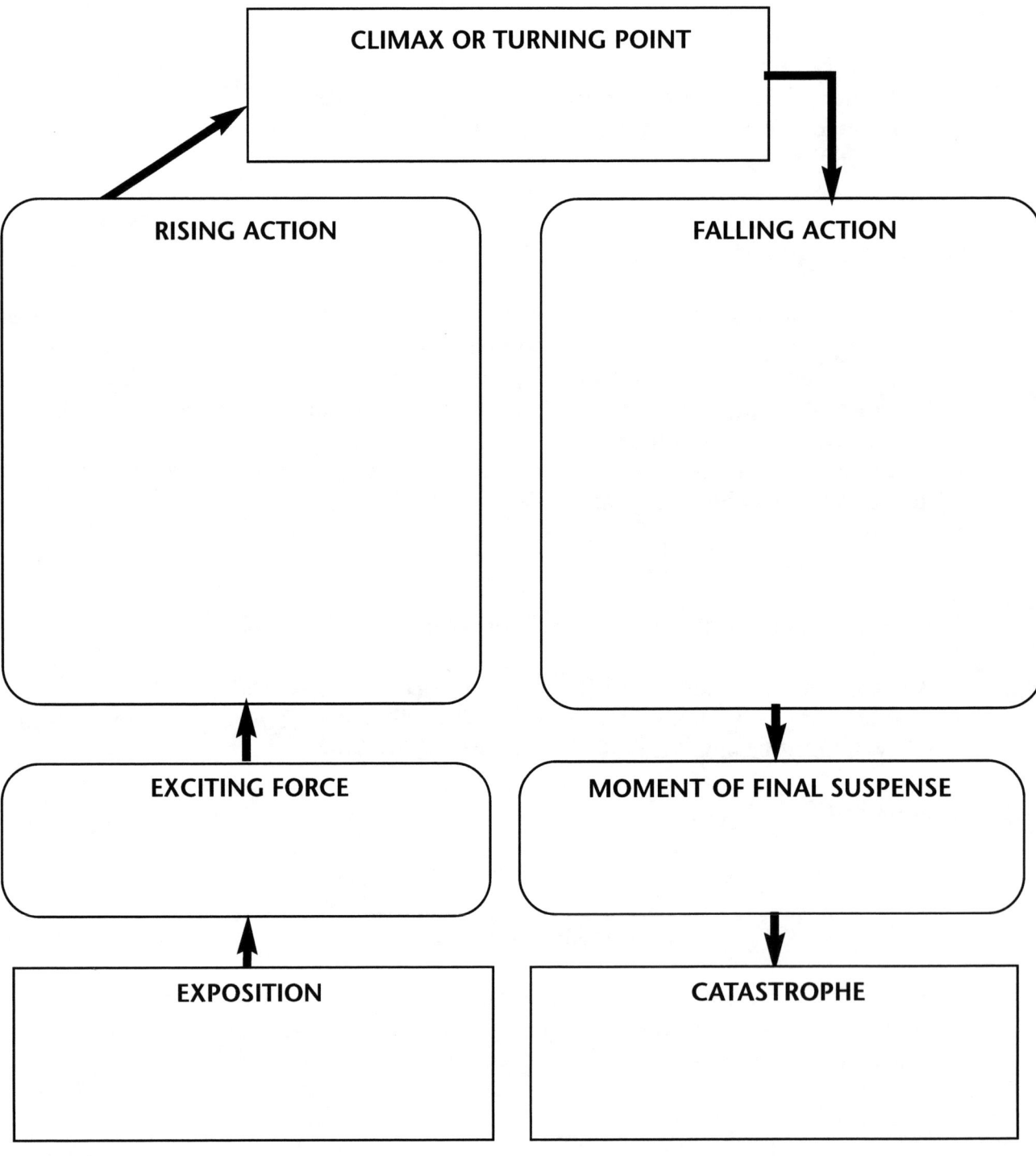

- *tragedy* - a serious play in which the protagonist fails to achieve his goals or i so overcome by the forces that are against him. The action usually ends with the protagonist's death, but in some plays he lives on, crushed in spirit and will. The protagonist suffers because he has rebelled against society or authority.

- *melodrama* - a serious play written to arouse the audience's emotions with bloodcurdling events, terrific suspense, and horrifying details. The plot often includes planned murders, defeated love and greed, and revenge. Character motivation and logical explanations are not necessarily important in melodrama; therefore, the audience does not question why things happen as they do. Good and evil are clearly defined in melodrama so that itis easy for the audience to identify the hero and villain.

Students will probably guess that *Julius Caesar* is a melodrama. Have them give examples from the play of the elements in the definition.

IDEAS FOR PROJECTS

1. As a research project, have students find out more about Julius Caesar and what actually happened during and shortly after his lifetime. They might then compare historical fact with Shakespeare's representation.

2. As an art/geography project, have a student draw a poster-size map of the Roman Empire in 44 B.C. This project can be assigned at the beginning of the unit so the map can be used as a visual aid.

3. As a drama project, have groups of students enact and videotape a soliloquy or a particular scene. This should be done as an outside project, but the finished video can be shown to the class.

4. Many famous sayings come from Shakespeare's plays. Have a student research these and write them on 6" wide strips of poster board that can then be placed around the room.

5. As an art/literature project, have a student draw a cartoon strip depicting an important scene from the play.

Assessment: Essay Topic Suggestions

1. In what way does the crowd function as a character in *Julius Caesar*?

2. One thing Caesar and Brutus have in common is their divided selves. Compare the two characters with special reference to their public and private selves.

3. Shakespeare often used imagery to create "mental pictures" in the mind's eyes of his audience. Give examples of this imagery.

4. Compare and contrast the scene between Portia and Brutus with the scenes between Caesar and Calpurnia.

5. Compare and contrast either of the following: Antony and Brutus; Cassius and Brutus.

6. Flattery is a tool used a number of times by characters in *Julius Caesar*. Give examples.

7. Compare and contrast the funeral orations for Caesar given by Brutus and Antony.

8. Define *dramatic irony* and give examples from the play.

9. Did Shakespeare provide credible motivation for the important steps taken by each of his major characters? Support your answer with details and examples.

10. What is the dominant theme of Julius Caesar? Support your opinion with details and examples.